14.95

Rivers and Lakes

Amazon River

Cari Meister

ABDO Publishing Company

visit us at
www.abdopub.com

Published by ABDO Publishing Company, 4940 Viking Drive, Edina, Minnesota 55435.
Copyright © 2002 by Abdo Consulting Group, Inc. International copyrights reserved in
all countries. No part of this book may be reproduced in any form without written
permission from the publisher.

Printed in the United States.

Photo credits: Corbis

Contributing editors: Bob Italia, Tamara L. Britton, Kate A. Furlong, Kristin Van Cleaf
Book design and graphics: Neil Klinepier

Library of Congress Cataloging-in-Publication Data

Meister, Cari.
    Amazon River / Cari Meister.
        p.   cm. -- (Rivers and lakes)
    Includes bibliographical references and index.
    Summary: Surveys the origin, geological borders, water, plant and
animal life, and economic and ecological aspects of the Amazon
River.
    ISBN: 1-57765-101-4
    1. Amazon River--Juvenile literature.   [1. Amazon River.]
I. Title. II. Series.
GB1258.M45 1999
551.48'3'09811--dc21   98-8662
                                                CIP
                                                  AC

Contents

The Amazon River

*T*he Amazon River is in South America. The river begins in Peru. From there, the river travels eastward across the continent and empties into the Atlantic Ocean.

Along its course, the Amazon River is joined by many **tributaries**. The tributaries add water to the Amazon. More water flows through the Amazon River than any other river on Earth!

The large area of land surrounding the Amazon River is important to the environment. This land is covered by the world's largest rain forest. It is rich in plant and animal life.

Today, the Amazon River and its rain forest are a mix of ancient and modern cultures. Many people worry that modern industries are hurting the Amazon River and its rain forest. Environmental groups are working to preserve this amazing area for the future.

The Amazon River is the second-longest river in the world. Only the Nile River in Africa is longer.

The Amazon's Course

*T*he Amazon River begins high in the Andes Mountains of Peru. There, snow on the mountaintops melts and forms the Apurímac River.

The Apurímac flows down the Andes and joins the Ucayali River. Then the Ucayali meets the Marañón River near Iquitos, Peru. When the Ucayali and Marañón Rivers meet, they form the **headwaters** of the Amazon River.

From its headwaters, the Amazon flows east for 4,000 miles (6,436 km). Along its course, more than 1,000 **tributaries** join the Amazon River. The tributaries come from Peru, Colombia, Ecuador, Bolivia, Venezuela, and Brazil.

At the end of its course, the Amazon River empties into the Atlantic Ocean. This takes place near Marajó Island, Brazil. There, the **mouth** of the Amazon River is nearly 40 feet (12 m) wide.

Amazonia

*T*he Amazon River is located in a low-lying area of land called a basin. The Amazon River Basin is often called Amazonia. It stretches across much of northern South America. It includes the Amazon River and all of its **tributaries**.

Amazonia is home to the world's largest rain forest. The rain forest is made up of trees, shrubs, vines, and flowers. It provides shelter for many different animal species.

Amazonia's climate is warm and humid. It is also very rainy. Each year, Amazonia receives between 60 and 120 inches (152 and 305 cm) of rain! The rain is especially heavy during the rainy season, which lasts from November to June.

During the rainy season, the Amazon River floods. Floods can cause the river's level to rise 50 feet (15 m)! This happens when the Amazon River is filled with **snowmelt** from the Andes Mountains and heavy rain at the same time.

Heavy rains fall over the Amazon and its rain forest nearly every afternoon.

Amazon Plants

*P*lant life in the Amazon rain forest grows in layers. The top layer is called the canopy. Most trees in the rain forest make up this layer. It receives lots of sunlight and rain. Sometimes, a few trees grow taller than the canopy. These trees are called emergents.

Below the canopy is the understory. Trees in the canopy shade the understory, so it receives little sunlight. Ferns, shrubs, vines, and palm trees grow well in the understory.

Below the understory is the forest floor. It receives hardly any sunlight. The forest floor is covered with branches and fallen leaves. They **decompose** quickly and provide minerals needed by plants.

For years, scientists have studied the layers of the rain forest and the plants that grow in them. Some of these plants have been helpful to humans as medicines. Scientists hope plants not yet discovered may provide cures for diseases such as cancer.

Layers of the Amazon Rain Forest

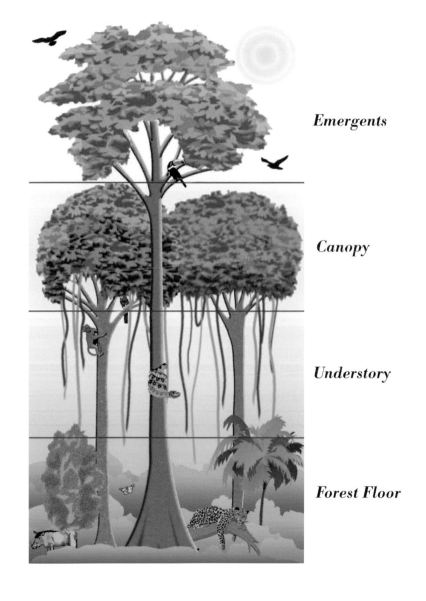

Emergents

Canopy

Understory

Forest Floor

Amazon Animals

*E*ach layer of the Amazon rain forest is home to different kinds of animals. Eagles, bats, monkeys, and sloths live in the canopy. Some of these animals spend their entire lives in the treetops without ever setting foot on the ground!

The understory and forest floor are also rich in animal life. Large animals, such as jaguars and tapirs, live in these layers. Spiders, beetles, butterflies, and frogs live in the understory and on the forest floor, too.

The waters of the Amazon River are also home to many animals. More than 1,500 species of fish live in the Amazon River. The piranha is one of the Amazon's most famous fish. Its razor-sharp teeth and strong jaws can quickly rip apart its prey.

The anaconda also slithers through the waters of the Amazon River. This snake can grow to be 40 feet (12 m) long! Anacondas are not poisonous. They kill their prey by crushing it.

Sloths eat, sleep, and mate without ever leaving the treetops!

The First Settlers

*F*or thousands of years, native peoples lived along the banks of the Amazon River and its **tributaries**. They were the first people to live on this land.

The native people survived by fishing, hunting, and farming. They traveled the Amazon River and its tributaries in dugout canoes and sailing rafts.

Native peoples used plants from the rain forest in their daily lives. For example, they used rain forest plants to create a drug that treats **malaria**. They also used plants to invent hammocks for sleeping and **blowguns** for hunting.

Opposite page: Some native peoples of the Amazon continue to follow the customs of their ancient ancestors, such as these Jivaro men who are using blowguns.

European Explorers

*I*n the 1500s, Europeans began exploring South America. A Spanish solider named Francisco de Orellana was the first European to discover the Amazon River. In 1541, he began his journey on a **tributary** in Peru. He sailed down the Amazon River until he reached the Atlantic Ocean the next year.

On his journey, Orellana met many native peoples. He claimed that one group he met was made up of tall, female warriors. They reminded him of a Greek legend about female warriors called Amazons. So Orellana called the land he discovered Amazon. Soon this became the name of the river, too.

After Orellana's journey, more Europeans began exploring the Amazon River. This made life difficult for many of the native peoples. The Europeans forced many native peoples into slavery. Others died from diseases carried by the Europeans.

In the 1870s, many European settlers moved to Amazonia in hopes of becoming rich. They wanted to make money by **tapping** rubber trees in the rain forest. The rubber industry became successful. Soon, other businesses began moving to Amazonia to make use of its many natural resources.

When a rubber tree is tapped, latex runs out. Latex is used to produce rubber.

Amazonia Today

*T*oday, more than four million people live in Amazonia. Most of them live in cities along the Amazon River and its **tributaries**. The major cities are Iquitos in Peru, and Manaus and Belém in Brazil.

Few roads link these cities. So people travel by boat. They use motor boats, canoes, and rafts. Large, oceangoing ships can also travel through the Amazon's deep waters.

Amazonia is home to many different industries. Loggers cut down trees in the rain forest. The lumber is used for building furniture and homes. Ranchers burn down trees in the rain forest. They use the land for fields and pastures. Miners drill the land in hopes of finding iron, gold, and oil.

Amazonia's cities and industries have grown. But some parts of Amazonia have remained unchanged. About 75,000 native people still live in the area. Many live in remote areas of Amazonia, far from busy cities and heavy shipping traffic.

The Amazonian city of Manaus, Brazil, is home to more than one million people.

Saving the Amazon

Recently, many people have become worried about the future of Amazonia. They fear that loggers, ranchers, and miners have cleared too much of the land. If this continues, many of Amazonia's plants and animals may become extinct.

Environmental groups are working to stop more damage to Amazonia. They want to preserve the river and the rain forest. These groups have had some success. National parks have been created in Peru, Ecuador, Colombia, Venezuela, and Brazil.

One of the most famous people to fight for the rain forest was a man named Chico Mendes. He grew up in the rain forest and worked as a rubber **tapper**. He organized a union to stop loggers and ranchers from clearing more land.

Some people disliked Mendes's work. They wanted to continue using the rain forest without worrying about the environment. So in 1988, a group of ranchers murdered Mendes. Though Mendes died, his work lives on in Amazonia today.

Chico Mendes

Glossary

blowgun - a tube through which a person blows darts or arrows.

decompose - to break down into simpler compounds.

headwaters - small streams that join to form a larger river.

malaria - a disease caused by mosquitos in tropical areas.

mouth - the location where a river empties into another body of water.

snowmelt - water produced when snow melts.

tap - to pierce a tree to let liquid drain from it. When people tap rubber trees, latex drains from the tree. Latex is used to make rubber products.

tributary - a river or stream that flows into a larger stream, river, or a lake.

How Do You Say That?

Apurímac - ah-poo-REE-mahk
Belém - beh-LEHM
Francisco de Orellana - frahn-SEE-sko day or-eh-YAH-nah
Iquitos - ee-KEY-tohs
Manaus - muh-NOWS
Marajó - mah-ruh-ZHO
Marañón - mah-rah-NYON
Ucayali - oo-kah-YAH-lee

Web Sites

Journey into Amazonia
http://www.pbs.org/journeyintoamazonia/explorer.html
This interactive site by PBS allows visitors to become Amazon explorers!

Rain Forest Alliance
http://www.rainforest-alliance.org/
This site has up-to-date information and news on the Amazon rain forest and fun activities for students.

These sites are subject to change. Go to your favorite search engine and type in Amazon River for more sites.

Index